Quotable ROCKNE

Quotable ROCKNE

WORDS OF WIT, WISDOM, & MOTIVATION BY AND ABOUT **KNUTE ROCKNE**, LEGENDARY NOTRE DAME FOOTBALL COACH

JOHN HEISLER

TowleHouse Publishing
Nashville, Tennessee

Copyright © 2001 by John Heisler

All rights reserved. Written permission must be secured from the publisher to use or reproduce any part of this book, except for brief quotations in critical reviews or articles.

TowleHouse books distributed by National Book Network, 4720 Boston Way, Lanham, Maryland 20706. (1-800-462-6420)

Library of Congress Cataloging-in-Publication Data is available.
ISBN: 1-931249-06-7

Page design by Mike Towle
Cover design by Gore Studio, Inc.
Cover photo: AP/Wide World Photos
Inside photos courtesy of University of Notre Dame sports information department.

Printed in the United States of America

1 2 3 4 5 6—05 04 03 02 01

CONTENTS

INTRODUCTION

Seventy years after his death stunned the nation, seventy-one years after his last Notre Dame team won a mythical national championship, eighty-three years after his first victory as the University of Notre Dame head football coach, Knute Rockne's legacy lives on.

It lives on in the person of Easter Heathman, one of the few individuals still alive who were there when Rockne's Fokker F-10 plunged into the earth near Heathman's home in Bazaar, Kansas. He's the unofficial tour guide to the spot where the plane crashed in 1931, prematurely snuffing out, at the tender age of forty-three, the life of the world's most famous college football coach.

It lives on at Highland Cemetery in South Bend, Indiana, where Rockne is buried next to his wife Bonnie. The grave site can be hard to find, but it remains a repository for flowers, handwritten notes, cigars, and other Notre Dame paraphernalia.

It lives on every spring when the Notre Dame Club of Saint Joseph Valley, the South Bend-area alumni club, holds its annual Rockne Mass and Communion Breakfast. The club's scholar-athlete award, presented every year in every varsity sport at Notre Dame, is named after Rockne, who was a chemistry professor at the University before he was a football coach.

It lives on in the form of a United States commemorative postal stamp that was issued with his likeness on it in 1988, a hundred years after his birth.

It lives on at the Rockne Memorial Building on the University of Notre Dame campus. Displayed prominently inside is a well-worn bust of Rockne. Former Irish coach Ara Parseghian was known to address it, "You started all this."

And so he did.

More than seventy years after he coached his last game for Notre Dame—his teams had won nineteen straight games and consecutive national titles at the time of his death—Rockne lives on in perpetuity. His spirit is as alive as ever. There's a Rockne Drive in South Bend close to the Notre Dame campus, and the Indiana Toll Road rest stop immediately west of South Bend bears his name.

Introduction

In the post-World War I era that segued into the Great Depression, at a time when heroes such as Babe Ruth, Bill Tilden, Jack Dempsey, Red Grange, Bobby Jones, and Walter Hagen captured the fancy of the sporting world, Rockne outdid them all in terms of popularity.

He did it by helping to put Notre Dame football on the national map. He had begun that task as a player, when in 1913 he starred as a receiver in a landmark victory against Army at West Point. As the Irish coach beginning in 1918 at the age of thirty, his teams were known as the Ramblers based on their coast-to-coast travels to play games.

Rockne's Notre Dame teams won games like no other dynasty in college football history. His thirteen-season career record of 105-12-5 (an .881 winning percentage) remains the best in the history of college football.

Rockne didn't just win games—he promoted college football like no one has since, building relationships with media and other key figures involved with the college game. The strong ethnic diversity of his Notre Dame teams was a perfect fit with the American immigrant population.

In 1999, *The Sporting News* ranked Rockne seventy-sixth on its list of the one hundred most powerful people in sports in the twentieth century, calling him "a tactical innovator and football's greatest motivator."

Known for bringing out the best in his players on the field, he charmed them with his oratory. His witty locker room comments remain at the heart of the Rockne legend.

He also had the pleasure of coaching some of the greatest players in the game. The star of Rockne's first Notre Dame team was the legendary George Gipp, who became Notre Dame's first All-American and remains, arguably, the greatest player in the history of college football. Like Rockne's, Gipp's life came to an untimely end when he died of a throat infection not long after his senior season in 1920.

The Gipp-Rockne legend lives on thanks to Gipp's deathbed plea of Rockne to tell one of his future Notre Dame teams to "win just one for the Gipper." Eight years passed before Rockne brought out the Gipp speech to use with his 1928 team prior to playing Army. The movie *Knute Rockne—All-American* made Hollywood heroes of Ronald Reagan as Gipp and Pat O'Brien as Rockne.

Rockne also coached the famed Four Horsemen—Harry Stuhldreher, Elmer Layden, Don Miller, and Jim Crowley—so dubbed by New York sportswriter Grantland Rice. The quartet also proved to be nearly unbeatable on the field, helping Rockne and Notre Dame win their first national championship in 1924.

The Gipp and Four Horsemen sagas remain two of the most romanticized epics in the lore of the college game.

Rockne's fame came about thanks to the on-field success of the Notre Dame shift. Off the field, he wrote his own newspaper column and helped design Notre Dame Stadium, which remains home for the Fighting Irish. At the time of his death, he was in great demand as a public speaker and corporate spokesperson.

Rockne's death in 1931 created such a national calamity that, as recently as March 2001, ESPN Classic did its own hourlong special on the plane crash, seventy years after the fact.

But Rockne lives in the dozens of books about him that have been written, from the time of his death until Ray Robinson's most recent 1999 biography, *Rockne of Notre Dame.*

He lives based on the legacy left behind for other Notre Dame football coaches to follow. For Parseghian, Frank Leahy, and Lou Holtz—the three Irish coaches whose tenures come closest to Rockne's in length—they needed all the passion and drive they could muster to enable their successes and championships to move them out of the lengthy Rockne shadow.

He lives in the handful of his former players still alive who can attest to his verve, his calculating style, his way with words, and his hands-on way with players.

Knute Rockne lives on.

Quotable
ROCKNE

MOTIVATION

1. We've come a long way down here in the South to play this game. We're meeting a great team in Georgia Tech, the greatest in the South. We're playing in a climate that is warm, new to us, and that may give us trouble. We're a young, green team. But now, I want you to show me what you're going to do for Notre Dame and for me and for yourselves. And remember, I don't want you boys to be the kind that are willing only to go out there and "die for Notre Dame." I want you to go out there this afternoon and live for Notre Dame. Remember that Georgia Tech will be playing this afternoon not only for Tech but for the honor of Southern football.

   —*before the 1922 Georgia Tech game*

2. I don't think a college football team can be brought to the top of its emotional pitch more than twice in a season of nine or ten games. If there are two games you've got to win, you can point for those, especially if one is the last game on the schedule. But you've got to take the others in stride.

3. Sure you are better, but you forgot to show him your newspaper clippings, and he doesn't know how good you are.

   —to a star tackle struggling against an opponent

4. One oration a season is quite enough for any football squad. If a coach talks too much, his words lose weight.

5. Come on, boys!

   —his pregame speech before the 1930 Army game

6. The freak psychologists will tell you that a shot of adrenaline will cure cowardice in the case of a football player who is afraid. The practical football coach knows that this is a lot of bunk. He knows that if a man is yellow, he is yellow, whereas the boy with character and willpower will overcome his fears and will go into the game showing those qualities we know as raw courage. Courage is largely a matter of breeding, environment, and development of the proper mental habits.

7. I have experienced the emotional reactions that come to a young player under one of those great oratorical coaches. In my first college game, we played a small college which came to Notre Dame with a very ordinary team, though we did not know it at the time. Just before game time the coach would peep in now and then and go away. But with each peep a cold shiver would run up my back. Finally, just after the bands had begun playing and the staccato cheering came faintly to our ears, the coach entered and, throwing his head back with a gesture worthy of Robert Mantell, began his speech. "Men of Notre Dame, today the eyes of a nation are upon you. Our alumni from Portland, Oregon, to Portland, Maine, are awaiting with taut nerves and bated breath the results of this contest. You will have to live up to the tradition of our fighting heroes of bygone years, in the days when men were real men. What are we going to show?" . . . He continued in this strain and then addressed each player personally. When my turn came I can still remember the words: "Are you going to lie down like a yellow dog this afternoon or are you going out for the old school and play like a fighting man?" I remember we left the dressing room growling to ourselves and what we did to the poor little Michigan College was nobody's business.

8. Playing with boys' emotions is a dangerous thing, and the coach who does so must pay for it. Of course, there are times when the whole season may depend on winning a certain game, and in that case many of the old-time coaches have resorted to psychological tricks.

9. So this is the so-called "Fighting Irish." You look to me like a lot of peaceful sissies. Well, I have been here too long to stand for this kind of nonsense and I quit—I resign right now! Tom (Lieb, assistant coach), take charge of the team. As far as I am concerned I never want to see any of you again, and in my mind your names will always be mud.

—halftime speech while trailing Northwestern, 10-0, in 1925 (Notre Dame won, 13-10)

10. About six years ago, our first big game of the season was with Georgia Tech. Winning the game was important, as the loss would probably mean that our green team might go to pieces for the rest of the season. So I determined to win the game, if possible. Just before the game I read several telegrams to the team and then one to the effect that my little boy Billy had suddenly become very seriously ill. Quite ill he was, in fact, and the telegram from my wife stated that the only thing that seemed to be worrying him was whether or not Daddy's team would win. She added, so I read the imaginary telegram, that she felt that if the team won it would be the best thing that could happen for poor little Billy. Needless to say the team went out keyed to a razor edge and the tackling was the talk of Atlanta for many a day. In fact, Red Barron fumbled seven times that day from the effects of just sheer wild crushing tackles. But I could never use any similar trick again. In fact, years afterwards, whenever I met any of the old team, their lips would break into a sardonic grin as they inquired: "Well, how is your boy Bill?" This was the first and last time I have ever used this sort of psychology.

11. Where's the boy who missed the kick? I'd like to meet him. Don't take it so hard, son. It's only a game and we had to be lucky to block the kick. Cheer up. This isn't the end of your life. It hasn't even started.

    —*to Army kicker Chris Broshus in 1930 after the Irish blocked a late PAT in a 7-6 win*

12. I had one team that was getting out of control. This team lost a game it should have won. I knew what overconfidence meant, so before the start of their next game I simply distributed newspaper clippings to the bunch. "Read these," I said. "These clippings say you're all All-America. But you couldn't beat a team last week that had no All-Americas. I want you to read these clippings before every play. Either you just aren't that good, or you're yellow."

13. Pardon me, girls, I thought this was the Notre Dame team.

 —another version of halftime at the 1925 Northwestern game

14. There has been a whole lot of water under the bridge since I first came to Notre Dame—but I don't know when I've ever wanted to win a game as badly as this one. I don't care what happens after today. Why do you think I'm taking a chance like this? To see you lose? They'll be primed. They'll be tough. They think they have your number. Are you going to let it happen to you again? You can win if you want to. Go out there and hit 'em! Crack 'em! Crack 'em! Fight to live! Fight to win! Fight to win . . . win . . . win . . . WIN!

 —pregame speech before 1929 Carnegie Tech
 game while stricken with phlebitis

15. So you're the Fighting Irish? What claim have you to that name? You look more like a bunch of lollipops to me. Here we are likely to lose the first game that has been lost on our home grounds in the last twenty-five years. That's a fine story that you'll be able to tell your children, grandchildren, and all generations to come. How you once had the "honor" of disgracing Notre Dame.

—yet a third version of halftime at the 1925 Northwestern game

16. The trouble with some of these young fellows is that they've been coached by their clippings and the opinion of the public. Soon they wise up and come around in line, all right. They're just a moving picture in human nature, that's all. Only sometimes they look like a Mickey Mouse animated cartoon and sometimes they look like a million dollars.

17. Losing that game did my team a lot of good. It was a game they figured to win. They eased up. They thought they could win at any time. In short, they thought they were better than they were. It was a good lesson, a chastening, humiliating lesson. They would never ease up again.

    —*on a 1923 loss at Nebraska*

18. That's when we go—that's when we lift our knees high and go inside of 'em and outside of 'em—inside of 'em and outside of 'em—that's when we charge down the field—that's when we go! Go! Go!

COMPETITION

19. They tell me I've got to take a rest. Perhaps I'll have to do as they say. . . . But it's a hard thing to do. You know you have to learn how to rest, and it's one of the toughest things I've ever tackled.

20. I don't like to lose. And that is not so much because it's just a football game but because defeat means the failure to meet your objective. I don't want a football player who doesn't take defeat to heart, who laughs it off with the thought that, *Well, there's another one next Saturday.*

21. The trouble in American life today, in business as well as in sports, is that too many people are afraid of competition. They are unwilling to make the sacrifice that means achievement and success. They are afraid to pit their resources against those of a competitor. The result is that in some circles people have come to sneer at success if it costs hard work and training and sacrifice.

22. I am not worried about boys when they are in school, in church, or with their Boy Scout Troop, or when they are home. But I am worried about them when they are playing. Their recreation can be either constructive or destructive.

23. Father, I'm not built for an invalid's routine. If you clip the wild duck's wings, he pines away and dies. I, too, must fly until I fall.

   —to Father Michael Mulcaire after Rockne
   was warned to follow a doctor's orders

24.

Everything worthwhile in life is gained through hard work, and I find resting up quite a task.

25. Everything else being equal, a football game is largely a contest of wits. A smart team is a team that is not fooled, but plays good, sound football all the time. The victory goes not only to the strong and brave—but to the smart team.

26. Plays do not mean so much on offense as one may think. One team will put on a play that works wonderfully. Another team will put on the same play and it will look terrible. It is all a matter of execution.

HUMOR

27. All right, boys; go to the showers now before Jack Cannon spoils any more plays.

   —during a midweek scrimmage

28. I'm going to call them "Minute Men," because they will be in the game about a minute before the other team scores.

   —on his 1928 team

29.
One loss is good for the soul; too many losses are not good for the coach.

30. Carberry! You keep on playing like that and you'll spend more time on the bench than any judge I know.

   —comments to Irish player Glen Carberry, who then became known as "Judge"

31. Boys, this is going to be easier than we thought. They aren't expecting us.

   —when an Indiana University student manager refused to let Notre Dame's team past the stadium gate

32. It doesn't seem like a good idea to me, putting clubs into the hands of so many Irishmen.

   —on the sport of hockey at Notre Dame

33. The qualifications for a lineman are to be big and dumb. The qualifications for a backfield man are just to be dumb.

34. Someone explain to Wilbur what this is all about. He's a new man—he's only been on the squad three years.

35. Nobody in that game has a sense of humor. They got me to talk at a basketball banquet once, and I was expected to tell some funny stories. The only one I could think of was that one of the basketball, which blew up and injured a lot of people. Do you know that basketball coaches were following me around for days afterwards asking me what there was funny about that?

—on the sport of basketball

36. On this play it was your duty, your quota, to do for him what he had done for you, namely take the Army right end out of the play and keep him out. But what did you do? You didn't even annoy him, and as a result (George) Gipp was thrown for a four-yard loss. As you lined up, quick as a flash Brandy called for the same play over again. He gave you a second chance to see if you would not do your bit for the team. But no, again you went out and leaned weakly against the Army end, who tossed you aside and threw Gipp for another loss. So I took you out. Now I am saving you. For the junior prom.

37. I was talking to a fellow scribe recently, and he wanted to know by what right I wrote about basketball. I replied that once upon a time I coached a basketball team. This is true. One winter, (Gus) Dorais, our regular basketball coach, became ill with the flu. There being no one else handy, I took over the team. I did the best I could. After winning the first game we lost the next eleven. We had just been beaten by Michigan State, making eleven losses in succession, and I was sitting in the hotel lobby feeling about as far down in the dumps, and looking it, as I could. At that Harry Mehre, present coach of football at the University of Georgia and the only basketball player on the team, by the way, came by and, slapping me on the back, said, "Don't feel so bad, coach, we can't win them all."

38. In fact, I sometimes feel that the alumni are impossible in their unfair demands for victory. I think it was Major Cavanaugh who once said that if he had his choice of coaching positions and the salaries were all the same that he would like to coach at Sing Sing. "The alumni very seldom come back, and when they do come back they are never noisy," Cavanaugh explained.

39. Handling the imprints of the townspeople on the mental attitude of the team is sometimes difficult. In fact, during every football season, I sometimes wonder why a college hires a coach when there are so many experts in town.

40. I found the criticism getting rather caustic one fall so I had to take heroic measures. Whenever I walked into the club or into the barbershop my daily greeting was: "And how are all the coaches today?"

41. My experience has been that the boys playing football take it no more or less seriously than they do anything else in their daily routine. . . . I remember well the third quarter of the Army–Notre Dame game of 1913. The score was 14 to 13 in Notre Dame's favor. West Point had just made a march which put the ball on our one-yard line. Just before the quarterback, Pritchard, began calling out his numbers, one of our linemen raised up and said: "Gee, that was a wonderful lunch we had; I wonder what we'll have for dinner." The West Point team relaxed from the humor of the remark and lost their chance to score at that particularly opportune moment. In fact, standing in the showers after the game the lads from both teams were exchanging banter, and this remark by our lineman came in for more than its share of laughter.

42. In one of the Nebraska games one fall, early in the third quarter, Griffith, I think it was, had been injured slightly, and I turned around to Barry, a little Irish halfback, with instructions to start warming up. In the excitement of the game I forgot Barry until it was all over. As I was standing around with the substitutes and managers picking up headgear after the game, Barry, dripping with perspiration, came to me and said, "My God, why didn't you put me in there?" I was nonplussed for a second until I realized I had left Barry warming up for a half hour, and then I said: "Couldn't you see why? (George) Gipp was the best man on the field and I couldn't take him out." "He may have been the best man on the field," said Barry finally, "but I was the hottest."

43. Protect yourself in the clinches but keep your mind on your work until the game is well in hand; then, if your adversary persists in the delusion that he is Jack Dempsey, disillusion him.

44. Forget it, son. You played well. There's only one favor I have to ask of you. Whenever you cross the goal line for a touchdown, always remember to take the ball with you.
    —*to Jim Crowley after he fumbled inside the two in a 0-0 tie with Army in 1922*

45. Well, Demosthenes didn't have any hair, either!
    —*on his premature baldness*

46. After I had taken him through twenty-five thousand miles of travel, he failed in geography.

—on his lone academic casualty at Notre Dame

47. Heads up there, Joe! They won't give you a chance to tie your shoes in the Army game!

48.

Bend your knees, Joe.
Throw away your
knitting needles and
get into the ball game.
Remember, this is
football, rough
but manly!

49. Joe, you're telegraphing your play. The purpose of a good offense is to deceive. Regardless of intent, keep your eyes glued on one spot on all plays. If you're going to give away a play, it'd be much better to send your opponent a postcard.

50. That's just fine. I was about to ask for it, anyway.

    —when a frustrated player threatened to turn in his uniform and quit

51. The genial Colonel blew his whistle so many times in the game that he kept right on blowing it in his sleep, and before morning five dogs had jumped in bed with him.

    —on one particular official from a game against Northwestern

THE GIPPER

52. Gipp was the greatest natural athlete I've ever seen. If you could get Gipp's interest aroused, there was no telling what heights he would reach. But getting his interest aroused was the trick! You couldn't get him to exert himself any more than he had to, and if the games in which he played happened to go Notre Dame's way without much of a struggle, I doubt if Gipp would ever have been considered much more than an average good football player. But let the game threaten to get out of hand and there was no stopping Gipp. He played like a man possessed, and he played until he expended every ounce of his great reserve power if the situation warranted. It seemed to me that anything Gipp made up his mind to do he could do and do better than anyone else. It wasn't necessary for him to have background or much preliminary work in any sport to get the hang of it. You did not have to tell him more than once what was the thing to do before he was doing it correctly. More often than not he did the correct thing as if instinctively.

53. George Gipp was the greatest
football player Notre Dame ever
produced. He was unequaled in the
game by anyone, save, perhaps, Jim
Thorpe. Gipp had everything to
make a man great—splendid
physique, balanced temperament, a
brilliant mind.

54. He accepted their congratulations
calmly, almost without reaction. It
wasn't quite natural. I wondered just
how unusual the kid was, and what it
would be like in the future, because
there was no doubt he was going to
be a world-beater—but a loner.

55. I came to know a lot—and yet little—about George Gipp. He lived quietly, but had no single close buddy, nor even a circle of good friends. He rarely dated a girl. And, to our disappointment, he skipped study room more than (Jesse) Harper and I liked. Yet it was impossible for anyone not to like him and enjoy every moment spent with him. He was pleasant—but never cheerful. Friendly but never overtly congenial.

56. He was in excellent physical condition, always, but there'd be times he'd come out of a game absolutely physically drained from exhaustion from putting out all he had. Yet he never allowed himself to lose complete control of his emotions. Perhaps if he were more emotional he could have risen to even higher heights than the incredible things he was able to do. I learned very early to place full confidence in his self-confidence.

57. George, George, where have you been?
    Now get over there with the sixth team.

    —when Gipp appeared for practice Wednesday
    after missing Monday and Tuesday

58. Gipp . . . was Nature's Pet. . . . he had the
    timing of a tiger in pouncing on his
    prey . . . he was a master of defense . . . not
    a single forward pass was ever completed in
    territory that he defended.

59. Forgive me for speaking in this proprietary, or
    at least paternal, way of the boy, because I
    felt the thrill that comes to every coach
    when he knows it is his fate and
    responsibility to handle unusual greatness—
    the perfect performer who comes along rarely
    more than once in a generation.

60. Before he died, Gipp said to me, "I've got to go, Rock. It's all right. I'm not afraid. Sometime, Rock, when the team is up against it, when things are wrong and the breaks are beating the boys, tell them to go in there with all they've got and win just one for the Gipper. I don't know where I'll be then, Rock, but I'll know about it, and I'll be happy."

—Gipp's deathbed speech to Rockne

THE FOUR HORSEMEN

61. That would be like trying to compare Julius Caesar with Napoleon. Both were military generals and the only real difference I can think of is that one wore a three-cornered hat.

    —on being asked who was the greater quarterback,
    Harry Stuhldreher or Frank Carideo

62. How it came to pass that four young men so eminently qualified by temperament, physique, and instinctive pacing to complement one another perfectly and thus produce the best coordinated and most picturesque backfield in the recent history of football—how that came about is one of the inscrutable achievements of coincidence, of which I know nothing save that it's a rather satisfying mouthful of words.

63. As a typical example of the work of a line, I will tell you just one incident which took place in the fall of 1924. We played Lombard in the opening game of the year. I started my second team. At the end of the first quarter the score was 0 to 0—Lombard had played the second team on even terms at least, or had a slight edge. As the second quarter started I put in a new backfield, which later achieved countrywide fame through the name given them by Grantland Rice—"the Four Horsemen." However, I continued to use the same second-string line which had played the first quarter—a line which was below average and had one or two real weak spots in it. How did the Four Horsemen react behind this inferior line? Well, four times Notre Dame had the ball and four times the Four Horsemen were held for downs, being forced to kick on each occasion on the fourth down. It was in about the middle of the second quarter and the Four Horsemen had yet to make a first down. In fact, they had yet to make any appreciable gain. The Lombard players were through and on them before they had a chance to get well started. I then put in Adam Walsh and the rest of the first-string line, which later became famous as "the Seven Mules." What happened after these men went in? In five minutes the Four Horsemen had marched the length of the field twice without being

seriously checked. They scored fourteen points without apparent effort. I think the experience must have been rather an eye-opener to the Four Horsemen. They comprised a wonderful backfield. I have never seen any better. But the line which played in front of them was a thing of beauty to watch and was justly entitled to half the credit.

64. If you were to ask me today what stands out in my mind regarding these four boys, I would tell you resiliency of mind and the spirit of cooperation. As a matter of fact, I had a fifth strong backfield that year which averaged 185 pounds and was tough and fast. The reason they sat on the bench that fall was due to the fact that they were four individuals suffering from charley horse between the ears and could not work together.

65. Adam, I'm starting the first-team backfield with the second-team line. It might teach those fellows that they can't do it alone. Remind them of it when you get in the game.

    —*to captain Adam Walsh before the 1924 opener vs. Lombard*

66. Notre Dame, with the Four Horsemen, was playing a powerful Army team. Stuhldreher was running the team at quarterback. He called two plays that were broken up. Harry couldn't see just who was doing the damage, so he called the same play again—and never left his position. He merely waited and watched. He saw one of the crack Army backs spoil the play again. Although it was fourth down, Harry again called the same play. But this time he took out that Army back with a terrific block, and we picked up fourteen yards. That was my idea of smart football.

67. The football epic of the Four Horsemen is the story of an accident. The four did not play as a backfield in their freshman year—remember, I had seen them in practice and survived the experience.

68. As real athletes it was hard to beat the Four Horsemen. Somehow they seemed to go whenever they had to. In their last year together I never saw a game that, in their own minds, there was any doubts about the result.

69. Okay, you can put the boys aboard, but God help you if they fall off and get hurt.

   —*on posing the Four Horsemen on horses*

70. They were all deadly tacklers, which delighted their teammates and me immensely. With all the publicity the Four Horsemen were getting, it was important that they prove themselves all-around players. And I'll add this: They had the same fluid, coordinating instincts on defense as they did on offense. And because they were such great pass defenders they made our six- and seven-man line work.

71. I thought they could be whipped into a combination of average players. Not much more than that at the time. That's all the dream I had of them then.

—*his early evaluation of the Four Horsemen*

Baseball great Babe Ruth shows off at Notre Dame in front of another 1920s sports icon.

NOTRE DAME

72. Don't ever pay any attention to rumors about me going elsewhere to coach. Notre Dame took me in as a poor boy years ago. It gave me the opportunity for an education. It enabled me to make good in a field I have chosen for my own. I am indebted to the school as long as I live. Nothing will ever tear me away, no matter what the inducements. When I quit coaching Notre Dame, I am through with football.

73. Freshmen get nothing but abuse at Notre Dame—but plenty of that.

74. That is not true. We get good material, but it's the tradition and environment that enabled us to build up some players beyond the average.

   —*on suggestions Notre Dame teams had a wealth of material*

75.
What's wrong with you Irish; do you work nights? You sleep out here all afternoon.

76. When one speaks of the Notre Dame spirit, however, what does he mean? To one who has ever been in contact with it, or under its influence, it will never be forgotten. Joy, hope, enthusiasm, normal confidence, faith, and the thrilling ecstasy of duty well done and fairly, are ever present on the campus. These are reflected more in the athletic contests because of their nature than in any other activity.

77. The school is confident of its teams—is behind its teams to a man—and every student fights just as hard as any member of the team. Yet they are courteous to the visitors and every student takes it upon himself to treat a visiting athlete just as though he were a guest in his own home.

78. If we win, we brag a little, but not much. If we lose, we buck up and shut up, principally the latter. A Notre Dame man may be down but he is never out, and that spirit of hope, faith, and determination to succeed is typically Notre Dame. You will find it present in certain amounts in every man who has ever been fortunate enough to study at the old school.

79. Will Rogers once asked me in jest whether I thought his son could make the Notre Dame team in case he attended our school. I replied very seriously, as is my wont, that I thought no doubt he could, being a chip off the old block. But that in order to make sure that the balance of power of the eleven would be maintained, I might have to change his name to Rogernahan, Rogerski, or even Rogeoli, depending upon which nationality I needed.

80. Another coach at a big university wrote me quite seriously that he thought the vogue at Notre Dame of using a lot of players was very unfair, particularly since his school only had thirty men on the football squad. I looked up their catalog and found they had seven thousand boys in school, and yet only thirty men on the football squad. Yes, I think something ought to be done about this.

81. I remember well the experience of Paul Castner, a back of the Notre Dame eleven some years ago. Paul looked like line material when he reported, yet in line play he seemed to lack something—he simply wasn't there, and I was about reconciled that this big, thoroughly likable chap just didn't have football "It." Then one day I tried him at passing and punting and he was a real find. Castner was a natural backfield man and he developed into one of the best all-around backs we have ever had. His kicking, passing, and running with the ball were all of a high order, yet if we hadn't found his specialties he would have been just another scrub.

82.

To hell with the guy who'll die for Notre Dame. I want men who will fight to keep it alive!

83. Other schools have material as good if not better. I think the West Coast and the Northwest produces bigger man [sic]. But there at Notre Dame the spirit of the school is ideal from the standpoint of a coach. There is no girl element to speak of. No co-eds. Most of the men live in dormitories, and all but seniors must eat at the school lunchrooms. Attendance schedules and scholastic schedules are rigid. And I have always made it a business to mind my own business, realizing that football is an extracurricular activity like publications, dramatics, and so forth.

84. I never have to appeal to the faculty for eligibility leniency for any player. The requirements are rigid enough so that the boneheads can't stay in school. We don't want them anyway. . . . The man who has to beg for football material, who has to go around checking athletes for scholastic eligibility when mentally they have none is a plain fool.

85. I know they are knocking. But that's all right. In my writing and in all the other work I have done in addition to coaching, I have been honest. I have written my own stuff for the papers. I have taught the best football I know in my coaching schools. I have been honest with Notre Dame, and I have considered that my first duty is to provide as well as possible for my family against the day when I won't be coaching football teams and they won't be buying my stuff in the newspapers and magazines. And when that day comes that they think another coach can do a better job, I intend to be able to say a pleasant good-bye and carry away with me as few worries as possible.

—on critics of his pursuits outside coaching

COLLEGE FOOTBALL

86. Football is not and should not be a game for the strong and stupid. It should be a game for the smart, the swift, the brave, and the clever boy.

87. We must guard against those who would turn football into a game for sissies.

88.

Outside the Church, the best thing we've got is good, clean football.

89. I have three sons, and I want them all to play football if they are able. I want them to learn the lessons of right living because no boy can play on a high school or college team who smokes or drinks or does anything else that might interfere with his fullest proficiency. He learns to take his hard knocks without squawking, without kicking, without knocking, and without being cynical. He learns to take them as a matter of course. He learns how to play his games with the proper value, and by proper values I mean trying to win just as hard as he can and if he does, not bragging. And should he lose, he learns no alibi. Nothing destroys character more than constant alibi-ing over failure.

90. Today modern invention has brought about
so many changes that we seem to be in a
constant state of flux. Two of the
improvements which will no doubt make
remarkable advances in the next ten years
are aviation and television radio. . . . There
is no question but that in a few years we
will be able to travel from Chicago to any
part of the United States in fifteen hours.
There is no question but that within a year
or so a man will be able to sit down at home
at his radio and not only hear an account of
the game but see it on television. . . . There
is no question, too, but that the rapid
transit strides made possible by aviation will
increase intersectional games, bringing more
color into the various college schedules.

91. Football will never become standardized. This is one of the reasons for its intense popularity. A lot of new angles and fancy dipsy-doo will come out each fall that will catch defensive teams napping and please the enthusiast.

92. Of course, when the team wins everybody talks about "we," but when the team loses then they mention "him"—that's me. However, I find that a lot of discussion and criticism of the team is a healthy condition. I would far rather have them panning and discussing me and the team than not mentioning football at all. This indicates a healthy interest which is what we all want.

93. These are dire days for the men who have charge of football tickets sales at universities. If a football coach loses, his name is mud, and if he wins he's a hero. Win or lose, the manager of ticket sales is always in a very unenviable position. He does not, nor will he ever, satisfy all the alumni. This is due to the fact that most alumni feel that it is all right for the other fellow to follow the regular procedure for getting tickets, but as for himself, it is not necessary because he is a privileged character. . . . The job of selling football tickets for a college football game is an impossible one. The manager of ticket sales hasn't a chance. Someone has to sit around the goal line or even behind the goalposts, and what they have to say about the blankety-blank hound who sold them their tickets has fortunately never been printed.

94. Big-money gamblers will ruin collegiate football if they are not stopped. I have as thick a hide as a rhinoceros for this species of poor sport, and the only regret I have is that they didn't lose more. . . . Furthermore, he is lacking in a sense of humor, for every time he loses a bet he wants to have the coach fired.

95. Football teaches a boy responsibility—responsibility as a representative of his college; responsibility to his teammates; and responsibility in controlling his passions, his fear, his hatred, jealousy, and rashness. Football brings out the best there is in one.

96. I don't know whether we ought to have spring practice this year or not. It might take too much time from your drinking and necking.

97. Where does the money go? Does the faculty get it, do the football coaches benefit from it, does it get into the hands of alumni? No, it does not. Most of it goes into the college treasury to help new facilities, build new dormitories, classroom buildings, and laboratory equipment. This gives the student body a more complete education. Football helps to carry other college sports as well as the intramural programs. Those big crowds are necessary for that to happen. There's nothing wrong with football or any phase of it. When people keep criticizing it, it's a sure sign that football is doing well. Football is a great game. If there's any harm coming from it, it's coming from the crowds who flock into the stands. Why blame the game? It's like the man with indigestion blaming the food instead of himself for overeating.

98. No matter if the fans are alumni, neighbors, or just plain customers at the gates, they seem to like bigger and better scores. For my part, they'll get the best games that can be given by the material in hand. But it is folly to pile up scores at the expense of weak opponents just to gratify the vanity of followers. It's unfair to the opposite team and to one's own players. A game won by a point is nonetheless won, and better to watch than a one-sided contest.

QUICK QUIPS

99. The pass, pass, pray, and punt system.

   —*on some teams' futile attempts to run a passing offense*

100. Egotism is the anesthetic that deadens the pain of stupidity.

101. In a crisis, don't hide behind anything or anybody. They're going to find you anyway.

102.

Humility is the lesson every athlete must learn in secret commune with his soul—or he gets it in big sour doses on the field as thousands roar.

103. You can't be a football player and a lover, too.

104. Drink the first, sip the second, skip the third.

    —*on cocktails*

105. Success is based on what the team does, not on how you look.

106. Let all your boys practice receiving passes as it is good practice for everyone and, besides, it keeps everyone busy and happy.

107. In the words of Theodore Roosevelt: "Don't foul, don't flinch; when you hit the line, hit it hard."

108. Kicking a football before it hits the ground is very much like playing golf—the younger you start, the better you become at it.

109. On the day of the game, everyone should be kept away from the team, including the well-wishers and the lip enthusiasts who claim they have $1.50 on the team.

110. Boys, there seems to be considerable dispute as to which part of the team is more important—the line or the backfield. I believe in settling such disputes in democratic fashion. So we'll take a vote on it. The line wins, seven votes to four. And don't you backs ever forget it.

111. An ordinary back can get the distance when the way is cleared.

112.
Be a good loser. Don't beef. But don't lose.

113. Football is a game played with the arms, legs, and shoulders, but mostly from the neck up.

114. It's up to you to show them what we've got. Let's get down to business and carry the mail.

115. I can tell you one thing twelve times. After that, you're on your own. There are some dumb people, then some dumber ones, then you come next.

116.
Love to block, and let them know that you like it.

117. Knock 'em up in the nickel seats!

—a favorite practice exhortation

118. If every player handles his man, the perfect play happens—which means a score.

119. That pass of Pop's (Warner, Stanford coach) was the greatest scoring play I've ever seen. Either he scored on it or we did.

120.
When the going gets tough, that's when we like it.

121.

Fight to win, boys.
Fight to win, but
make fair play an
obsession.

COACHING

122. Halfbacks are born. Some coaches take a lot of credit for having developed certain halfbacks. What is generally meant by that is that a man with a lot of talent comes to a coach, and the coach does him no particular harm.

123. They lateral-passed Notre Dame out of the park. . . . It was the most valuable lesson Notre Dame ever had in football. It taught us never to be cocksure. Modern football at Notre Dame can be dated from that game. On the following Monday Jesse Harper put in the backfield shift, with my idea of shuttling or flexing the ends.

—on a 28-0 loss to Yale in 1914

124. I am running this team. Nobody else has anything to say about its makeup or play. If it's a flop, pan me. If it's a success—well let them say what they choose. I have worked around here as an assistant for four years and seldom have seen my name in print.

125. Out at Notre Dame we have our "control plan"—only we call it our "chart of play." If I had to coach football without it, I would probably quit coaching. This chart tells us everything we want to know about what happened in previous games—and shows us just where we can improve on the individual performance of every man. . . . How many times did Brill carry the ball, and how much did they average on each attempt? . . . On the plays that failed, which man is responsible, who failed to function 100 percent? . . . When we got to the goal line, why didn't we score? . . . What individuals fell down in picking off the secondary and safety men? Our chart tells us. Sometimes we feel like tossing that chart away and saying, "Oh, well, we won again, we've got a good team, and we ought to win again next week." But we've learned, by sad experience, that in competition as keen as modern football, we can't keep winning unless we keep improving—and we can't improve unless we have the facts—all the facts about every player and every department of play.

126.
The toughest poison a coach has to face in football is overconfidence.

127. Our system came from Adam. I learned it from Jesse Harper when he was head coach at Notre Dame, and Jesse learned it from (Amos Alonzo) Stagg when he was at the University of Chicago. Stagg brought it from Yale where he learned it from Walter Camp, and Walter learned it from Adam. So you see, there is nothing original about it as far as I am concerned, and it certainly goes back a long way.

128. Whenever I find any young fellow who is a chronic whiner and disturber, who insists on blaming his own shortcomings on his coaches and teammates—never on himself—we take the shortest way out. The next day that young chap comes out for practice, there is no suit in his locker. I hope the shock has done him good.

129. In these modern days of hard schedules, the boys on the team develop their own zest to win, to do the best they know how. All the coach does is to teach them how to play football and to impress on the boys the fact that they have a very hard game coming on.

130. Regarding the faculty, the coach should show the teachers early that he appreciates the fact that the boys are in school to study and that athletics are extra curricula. By keeping after his men about standing high in their class work, he can show the faculty that he sincerely appreciates the welfare of the boy more than he does merely winning games. A fair-minded faculty man will always reciprocate by cooperating with the coach when he sees that a proper balance is being maintained between the academic work and athletics.

Rockne in 1928 is joined in front of the Notre Dame Cathedral in Paris by his agent, Christy Walsh, and legendary coach Pop Warner.

131. I went downtown and dissolved my Committee of Sunday Morning Field Generals. The Committee was composed of the head barber, a sporting dentist, a bank president, and the night clerk at the hotel. They had been quite a help in telling me on Sunday morning what I should have done on Saturday. . . . I appreciated that the team and myself had to play Saturday's stock market on Saturday, figuratively speaking, whereas the Committee insisted on the right to play Saturday's stock market on Sunday. Dumb as I am, I figured I could do that myself.

132. The average professor goes into a classroom, gives his lecture, and leaves. His attitude is distinctly "Take it or leave it." He may flunk half the class and everyone is awestricken. The coach, however, has to be a super-teacher. He must see to it that the class learns what he has to teach. If he flunks half the class, he flunks with them. It is not what a coach knows, it is what he can teach his boys, what he can make them do.

133. Don't criticize one another and look for faults. All of us have plenty of faults. Let's get more fun and more team play by looking for the good points of our teammates.

134. Don't forget that eleven wide-awake boys who have their heads up, using their eyes to see, and with their minds active, are pretty hard to beat. Eleven smart boys, everything else being equal, will decisively beat eleven boys who are dull mentally and who do not use their eyes.

135. Know when to play it safe, know when to take a chance, know when to play it fast, know when to play it slow. Know which to do, and do it.

136. Several years ago I was unable to accompany the Notre Dame team to Pittsburgh, and we were beaten by Carnegie Tech in a manner that was more or less unexpected. The next week, in talking to one of our South Bend citizens, this man said, "Well, I see the boys couldn't do their stuff so well when the trainer wasn't present." He intended this as a compliment, but I did not take it as such. I was immediately reminded of an animal act in a circus. In this act, of course, the animals will not do their stunts unless the trainer is present to crack the whip, or to dole out lumps of sugar. I certainly can see no analogy between an animal act and a football team. . . . The test of education is whether the boys continue to do the right thing when the coach is absent.

137. Hot towels applied as hot as you can stand them will be found a great relief to most bumps and bruises. However, don't be a mollycoddle—remember that football is supposed to bring out the Spartan in the young boy, which means to make as little out of an injury as possible, not losing, however, the common-sense point of view.

138. I played on the Notre Dame football team in the years 1911, 1912, and 1913, and during those three years we never once scouted an opponent. Incidentally, we were undefeated those three years. The point I wish to make is that the lack of scouting in no way interfered with our efficiency. I believe most football coaches will agree that they could get along very well without scouting. . . . You may ask if it be better to play without knowing the other team's formations. Yes, but the knowledge of what formations they are using becomes so obvious that if we didn't send a scout out to see the other team play on Saturday and get the formations openly and honorably, the information would be bootlegged to members of the team by some underhanded method. Alumni and traveling salesmen with valuable football information are always hard to handle.

139. Overconfidence comes after success and means self-satisfaction, lack of interest, underestimating the opponent, and general mental dry-rot. It is the most difficult thing for the coach to handle but it can be handled in a football team as well as in any group of human beings. . . . Some chance remark may help to make this team overconfident, and an overconfident team is easily beaten by anyone. It is the worst possible mental condition.

140. I wish you fellows would be as strict as possible today. Since this is our opening game, I don't want my players to get into bad habits. Besides, I don't want to roll up the score. I won't even object if you call penalties that haven't been earned.

—to the officials before a 1919 game against Kalamazoo

141. Keep your eyes open. Keep your weight forward and low. Get your man right, and hit him. Don't slide up on him like he was a polecat. Crack it to him with your shoulders right at his hips. Then whip your arms around his legs and bend them out from under him. When his feet leave the ground he'll quit running. Keep your feet on the ground if you can. Don't make a flying tackle unless you have to; they're no good as a rule. Keep your feet on the ground and shove.

142. A coach's greatest asset is his sense of responsibility—the reliance placed on him by his players. Handling your personnel is the most important phase of coaching. The secret of coaching success can be reduced to a simple formula: strict discipline in your training program and on the field, combined with a high and continuing interest in all your other relationships with your kids.

143. One who in his playing days had to fight for everything he got.

—his description of the ideal coach

144. If you can't keep quiet, get out! I don't come into your classroom and laugh at your methods and results. This is my classroom!

—his response to outside kibitzers who criticized his coaching

145. Bask in the sunshine of a winning schedule, a difficult schedule—and those are the only schedules worthwhile, for "buffer" or rest games induce a letdown that, in turn, brings casualties—win your way through a half a dozen tough assignments, and just as you are congratulating yourself on results, some busy soul is preparing a brickbat to aim at your lifted head.

146. Some day there will be an exhibit in some American museum. It will be the forlorn figure of a coach who pleased nobody. And next to it will be another—and more forlorn exhibit—the preserved remains of the coach who tried to please everybody.

PHILOSOPHY

147. No matter how good a ball carrier a man is, he should not be allowed to play unless he also knows how to interfere and block. I would rather have a good interferer than a good ball carrier, insofar as the team is concerned.

148. A boy who hopes to be a good football player must have brains, courage, self-restraint, fine muscular coordination, intense fire of nervous energy, and an unselfish spirit of sacrifice. He must live cleanly. He must develop the will to win so keenly that he can taste it.

149. Men will work twice as hard under the stress of emotion as they would otherwise.

150. Never ridicule a beginner—you can kill talent before it blossoms.

151. The one thing no one can ever take away from you is your integrity.

152. The secret of winning football is this: Work more as a team, less as individuals. I play not my eleven best, but my best eleven.

153. That most base of emotions—hatred—does not enter into our athletic contests. Instead, the spirit is one of exhilaration, in joy of a contest well fought between men.

154. Pick the right men, teach them how to do things perfectly, then make them practice, practice, practice.

155. I could make a touchdown, old as I am, if each of you fellows carried out his assignment on the play.

156. Go out and win, but remember that we want no boasting if we are successful and no alibis if we lose. Give the other fellow credit if he is better than you are.

157. You know, all this hurry and battling we are going through is just an expression of our inner selves, striving for something better. The way I look at it is that we are all here to try to find, each in his own way, the best road to our ultimate goal. I believe I have found my way, and I shall travel it to the end.

—*on why he converted to Catholicism*

158. The Notre Dame system is based on speed and deception . . . Notre Dame shifts just the backfield and the two ends. The team can shift into one of eight variations off the same formation. Blocking is entirely a matter of having the proper angle. The main idea of the shift is to place men in position where they get the proper blocking angle on the defensive linemen. The proposition becomes more a matter of finesse than of bruising. . . . If this isn't smart football, then I'll eat your new fall hat without catsup.

159. One of the most difficult accomplishments I know is for the average football fan to learn any football. The average fan who watches a game loves to watch the ball and the ball carrier, and no doubt he gets an immense thrill now and then by doing so. It is my personal opinion, however, that he would get much more real enjoyment out of the game if he knew just a little more about the inside of the game. When it comes to the three backs who are not carrying the ball, and also when it comes to line play, I find the average fan is woefully lacking in any knowledge as to what's going on. He wouldn't be able to observe it if he did see it because it would mean nothing to him.

160. A successful football team must build up a tradition of giving praise not to the ball carrier but to the interferer and to the blocker; not to the star, in the popular sense, but to the man who can tackle and the man who can knock down forward passes.

161. Then take the poor, lowly guard—the martyr of the team. On offense the guard must pull out quickly and precisely; he must stay down low, like a bloodhound following the trail, and then cut around the defensive tackle and pick off the defensive fullback with the precision and accuracy of a bayonet man. The defensive fullback is the main cog in the defense, and if the offensive guard can clear him out of the way the play gains ground. If he doesn't, the play does not gain ground. The offensive guard makes an off-tackle play 35 percent better when he performs his job well. Does he receive any cheers from the crowd for his clever bit of work? He does not. He must be satisfied with the appreciation of his coach and his teammates.

162. Hunk Anderson and Pop Warner were holding a coaching school at Notre Dame. The group of coaches at Notre Dame was very much interested in the discussion between Pop and Hunk on the relative merits of the double-wing system and the shift. When the smoke all cleared away and the discussion was over, nothing had been settled except that it is up to each man to go out and coach football as he sees it and to create new ideas along his own individual lines. When the session broke up one evening at midnight, Pop, as a last argument, propounded the question, "Why do you shift?" And Hunk immediately came back with the query, "Why do you use two wing backs? Why does a base runner steal a base? Why does a pitcher use a curve ball? Why does a fast forward dribble around a sluggish stationary guard? Why did Corbett dance all around so Sullivan couldn't hit him?" And that was the finish of the discussion.

163. And don't forget that the only way to attain perfection is to keep on practicing until it becomes a habit, whether it is teaching charging, teaching blocking, or any of the hundred things that have to be learned and have to be performed if the boy is to be able to play the game of football well.

164. There must be no eating between meals, with the possible exception of some fruit before retiring at night. On the day of the game the boy should eat a good-sized breakfast. The meal just preceding the game, however, should consist of nothing but tea and a little toast. It is well to remember that most world's records have been made on an empty stomach.

165. A boy who starts practice fat, soft, and out of condition, because he hasn't been doing anything all summer, will also have to work easily. . . . A boy who reports in fair condition will find that two weeks of light work is about all he needs to keep in condition.

166. You must have a running attack and be able to defend against a running attack. This means that the boy must be able to block and tackle. Interference is nothing but collective blocking.

167. A number of coaches use a lot of rigmarole and artificial apparatus to try to teach the various stunts in football, but I don't believe in them. Their greatest value lies in publicity and advertising, and coaches who do not use these devices get better results when it comes to actually playing football. However, a football team which is practicing should work on the things which, as individuals, they must perform in the position they are playing in the game. They should become very proficient in every detail of their position. A chain is no stronger than its weakest link.

168. The same system holds true with the guards in teaching them their position, and, in fact, holds good for every position. First— They are told in simple, graphic language. Second—They are shown. Third—They perform. Fourth—They are criticized constructively. Fifth—They practice for perfection.

169. The open-field block, used against a defensive player who is running, is called the running dive with a roll. . . . If the boys all become proficient in these types of blocking, the team should be a dandy.

170. Sleep is a builder of tissue, fellows. This four-hour stuff the scientists are yelping about is great for guys like Edison. But Thomas Alva never galloped over a goal line with the pigskin. The more you get the clearer your eyes and the better your noodle works. You'll want the reserve it builds when you've got to out-burn a good backfield getting to the line first. Don't forget it.

171. An automobile goes nowhere efficiently unless it has a quick, hot spark to ignite things, to set the cogs of the machine in motion. So I try to make every player on my team feel he's the spark keeping our machine in motion. On him depends our success and victories.

172. We aim for maximum deception. Seeing our shift going to the right, the defense will go to its left, but the odds are the defense will shift too far, not far enough, or not quickly enough. No matter which, our offense has strategic points of attack opened up for it. In concentrating its strength to its left, the defense leaves its right greatly weakened, and before it has time to figure out where we're going, the ball has been snapped and the play is gone. And if they overshift to our strong side, we'll just come back with weak-side stuff and catch 'em where they ain't.

173. The use of dirty tactics is an open admission that you were weaker than your opponent, that you weren't able to battle him on even terms. If there's any fighting to be done, fight with your heart and mind rather than your fists and mouth.

174. It's good to be confident. I wouldn't give much for the boy who wasn't. You've got to get the most out of every minute of the day because opportunities don't come often. But any time you're inclined to slow up, or get filled with your own importance, take out your watch and remember that when that second hand moves from sixty to sixty, that minute is gone. If you have wasted it, it will do you no good, because it is gone, never to come back. But, if you've taken advantage of it, you can say, "I've made the best of my time."

175. Isn't it far better to have a group of boys working off their excess energy, after hours of classroom work, on the football field, under capable instruction in organized athletics, than it is to have the same young men dashing around in automobiles, cluttering the street corners or poolrooms or the drugstore?

176. Just because the Kaiser called them shock troops doesn't mean that we can't apply the same principle to the football field. You call 'em anything you want. We like what happens.

—*on starting the second team in games*

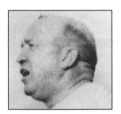

QUARTERBACKS

177. My quarterback would not be out there if I didn't think his tactics were sound. He sees the weak spots in a defense, and he knows what to do. If he doesn't, he doesn't belong. But for me to try to run the game from the bench would not only be unfair but unwise from the point of view of good football.

178. But, for goodness sake, don't allow the boy to play quarterback who is suffering from inferiority complex, who has no drive, or who is inclined to get panicky or excited in a pinch. These types of boys may play football at some other position but not at quarterback.

179. The coach can help the quarterback here immeasurably if he will sit down sometime after the quarterback has learned his plays fairly well and classify these plays according to the following table or something similar to it:

First—The strongest plays.

Second—Short sure gainers which are also good for one to three yards and which safeguard possession of the ball.

Third—Check plays.

Fourth—Gamble plays.

Fifth—Position plays.

Sixth—Sideline plays.

Seventh—Goal-line plays.

Eighth—Psychological plays.

Ninth—Trick plays.

Tenth—Time-killing plays.

Eleventh—Sacrifice plays.

Twelfth—Long gainers.

Thirteenth—Change-of-pace plays.

Most plays in the repertoire will, of course, be found under three or four of these classifications, but I do believe that this kind of a classification will immeasurably increase the quarterback's sense of values.

180. Tactics and strategy are of importance, and I will outline here just a few hints for the quarterback so that he will avoid mistakes which may boomerang against his team:

1. Know when not to forward pass.
2. When in doubt, punt.
3. Have confidence—believe in yourself.
4. Bark out your numbers distinctly and loud.
5. Be boss of the team.
6. If it looks as though a punt is going to roll for touchback, don't try to catch it.
7. When close to your own goal line, kick on first down unless you want to play for position.
8. If near the sideline, don't kick, but run a play for position.
9. When you discover a weak spot in the opposing line, don't forget it.
10. Remember what plays have been working and what plays have not been working.
11. Against a very strong defensive team, kick, kick, kick, and play for a break.
12. On a wet, muddy field let opponents carry the ball and do the fumbling; let us kick, kick, kick.
13. Always have lots of ginger, pep, and enthusiasm, and don't bawl anybody out. Instead, encourage everybody.
14. If worried, hide it.

15. Always be sure every player on your team is ready before you call a play.

16. Maneuver so as to keep away from the sideline; stay in the middle of the field as much as possible.

17. Look over the defensive team carefully and play the defense.

18. Watch who makes the tackle, and it may suggest a play to you.

19. Use punt formation deep in your territory. Save your close attack until you get past the middle of the field.

20. Stall against the wind and run plays quickly with the wind.

21. Stall when you are ahead; run plays quickly when you are behind.

22. Save your best forward pass plays for the second half.

23. If you have a weak kicker, try a long forward pass in your territory.

24. Against a team which has a powerful offense, hold the ball as long as you can.

25. Don't try to handle a kicked punt which is rolling uncertainly.

26. When catching a punt and you see the opponents have their ends right on top of you, signal for a fair catch.

27. When playing safety on defense, play safe. Observe and let nothing escape your attention.

28. Cover the long man with forward passes.

29. Be sure that you are able to tackle in the open, though if you can maneuver any ball carrier who comes through to you towards the sidelines, try and do so, as this will give him but one direction to go.

30. Learn to relax, stay cool, and retain your mental poise regardless of the excitement.

31. In offensive territory use your best play on first down, that is, your biggest ground gainer.

32. Try a trick play or "long gainer" after recovering a fumble, as the defensive team will then be in the air.

33. Watch for the psychological moment to pull your trick play.

34. When defensive line tightens up, use end runs; when defensive line is spread, use line plunges.

35. Keep in mind the tactical situation and play the defense.

36. Study your plays, your teammates, and the opponents, and there is no reason why you shouldn't be a good quarterback with a good sense of tactics. A good quarterback will lead his team to victory over physically superior teams, which, however, lack a tactical mind.

181. I'm not asking you to put on phony airs. You're just playing a role. It isn't you personally who I want to be cocky. It's you the Notre Dame quarterback. But be wise enough to know a limit. Don't get your own teammates soured on you. But you can irritate the opposing team all you want—the more the better.

OTHERS ON ROCKNE

ROCKNE CONDUCTED A COURSE THAT WAS ONLY INCIDENTAL IN EDUCATION. YET HE HAD A NAME AND FAME WITH THE UNDERGRADUATE WORLD AND THE PUBLIC SURPASSING THAT OF ANY FACULTY MEMBER IN THE COUNTRY. HIS ACTIVITIES HAD THE BENEFIT OF PUBLICITY, BUT THAT DOES NOT ACCOUNT FOR HIS HOLD ON YOUNG MEN. WE SHALL FIND THAT IN HIS CONSTANT DEMAND FOR THE BEST THAT WAS IN THEM. NO BLUFF WOULD ANSWER. FIFTY PERCENT WOULD NOT DO. HIS PASSING MARK WAS ONE HUNDRED. HE REQUIRED PERFECTION. THAT WAS WHY MEN LOVED AND HONORED HIM. THAT WAS THE SOURCE OF HIS POWER.[1]

—Calvin Coolidge, upon Rockne's death

RHYTHMICAL TEAMWORK, PAINSTAKING DETAILS, SELF-SACRIFICE, SPIRITUAL IMPULSE, AND LOYALTY WERE THE OCTAVES UNDER THE COMPLETE MASTERY OF THIS BEETHOVEN OF MODERN FOOTBALL.[2]

—Major Ralph I. Sasse,
U.S. Military Academy football coach

126

HE KNEW FOOTBALL PROBABLY AS NO ONE ELSE KNEW IT, BUT I AM CONVINCED THAT THIS WAS A MERE INCIDENT. HE SUCCEEDED AS HE DID BECAUSE HE SO ENDEARED HIMSELF TO HIS BOYS, INSPIRED THEM, LOVED THEM. FEW OF US REALIZED AT THE TIME THAT HE WAS TRANSPLANTING HIS SPIRIT, HIS VERY SOUL INTO EACH OF US. WORK, WORK HARD, PREPARE YOURSELF, THEN GO.[3]

—Adam Walsh, 1924 Notre Dame football captain

I THINK I HAVE HEARD FEW MEN WHO COULD SO STIR AN AUDIENCE, BOTH THROUGH HIS HUMOR AND HIS TRENCHANT, FORCEFUL PHILOSOPHY.[4]

—Glenn "Pop" Warner, Stanford football coach

I'LL ADMIT THAT JUST BEFORE HIS DEATH, I FELT TOWARD ROCK JUST AS I DID THE FIRST YEAR I MADE THE TEAM. CALL IT HERO WORSHIP OR NOT, THERE IT WAS AND I'LL ADMIT NOW THAT I'M NOT ASHAMED OF IT AND NEVER WILL BE. . . . THAT'S NOT BECAUSE HE WAS A GOOD, OR A GREAT, FOOTBALL COACH. BUT IT'S BECAUSE I AND MOST OF THE OTHER MEMBERS OF THAT SQUAD USED TO GO TO HIM WITH CONFIDENCES THAT WE WOULD NOT HAVE MENTIONED TO OUR OWN PARENTS. I KNOW THIS SOUNDS A LITTLE YOUNG, BUT IT'S TRUE.[5]

—A Four Horsemen-era Notre Dame lineman

127

THERE WAS ONE (SPEECH) THAT WAS A CORKER. IT WAS MADE BY A STOCKY, BALD-HEADED FELLOW WITH A NOSE THAT LOOKED AS IF IT HAD BEEN BROKEN. HE HAD A GREAT VOICE AND HE COULD PUT HIS STUFF OVER. HE HAD ME SITTING BACK AND LAUGHING ONE MOMENT AND LEANING FORWARD TO GET WHAT HE WAS SAYING THE NEXT. I WAS SITTING AWAY BACK IN THE REAR OF THE PLACE, AND I DIDN'T CATCH HIS NAME WHEN THEY INTRODUCED HIM. SOUNDED LIKE SOME SORT OF FOREIGN NAME. BUT HE SURE COULD TALK. I'LL HAVE TO FIND OUT WHO HE WAS.[6]

—an automobile dealer who heard Rockne speak

HE HAD A MIND THAT TOUCHED GENIUS, A BLOWTORCH SPIRIT, PHYSICAL COURAGE, INFECTIOUS HUMOR, RARE CHARM. . . . HE WAS A BATTLEGROUND OF EMOTION AND INTELLECT, OF MOODS AND FEUDS. HE COULD BE PETTY, SECRETIVE, SUSPICIOUS; BUT THERE WAS IN HIM NEITHER MALICE NOR HATE; AND MOSTLY HE WAS NAIVE, GENEROUS, KIND. HE USED HIS VOICE AS A WEAPON OR A SEDATIVE. HIS EYES COULD EXPRESS THE SIMPLE CHARM OF A CHILD, OR A TERRIFYING INNER FORCE.[7]

—author Francis Wallace

MR. ROCKNE SO CONTRIBUTED TO A CLEANNESS AND HIGH
PURPOSE AND SPORTSMANSHIP IN ATHLETICS THAT HIS
PASSING IS A NATIONAL LOSS.[8]

—President Herbert Hoover

IN A DAY OF SO MANY DISTURBING CHANGES IN OUR
NATIONAL LIFE, OF A GROWING INDIFFERENCE TO OLD-TESTED
STANDARDS IN PERSONAL AND PUBLIC LIFE, HAS
TENACIOUSLY ROCKNE CLUNG FAST TO FUNDAMENTALS. . . .
IN A DAY WHEN THE OUTLOOK OF SO MANY—YOUNG PEOPLE
ESPECIALLY—WAS TOO OFTEN CLOUDED BY SHODDY
PHILOSOPHY AND CHEAP CYNICISM, HOW ELOQUENTLY
ROCKNE HELD THAT LIFE WAS SOMETHING TO SEIZE UPON
JOYOUSLY AND MAKE ONE'S OWN. . . . HE LOVED YOUNG MEN
AROUND HIM AND WHAT HE CALLED THEIR "WARMTH OF
ACTIVITY." HE LOVED WIT AND LAUGHTER. HE LOVED THE
GREETINGS OF FRIENDS. HE LOVED HIS HOME. HE LOVED ALL
THE GOOD THINGS OF LIFE. NO MAN EVER COMMUNICATED A
GREATER ZEST FOR LIVING.[9]

—the Rockne Memorial Association

I NEVER KNEW MR. ROCKNE. I NEVER SAW HIM. BUT HE HAS BEEN MY INSPIRATION ALL MY LIFE. I FELT I HAD TO COME TO HIS FUNERAL.[10]

—an unidentified boy from Pittsburgh

IN AN AGE THAT HAS STAMPED ITSELF AS THE ERA OF THE GO-GETTER—A HORRIBLE WORD FOR WHAT IS ALL TOO OFTEN A RUTHLESS THING—HE WAS A GO-GIVER—A NOT-MUCH-BETTER WORD, BUT IT MEANS A DIVINE THING. HE MADE USE OF ALL THE MACHINERY AND THE LEGITIMATE METHODS OF MODERN ACTIVITY TO BE ESSENTIALLY NOT MODERN AT ALL; TO BE QUITE ELEMENTARILY HUMAN AND CHRISTIAN, GIVING HIMSELF, SPENDING HIMSELF LIKE WATER, NOT FOR HIMSELF BUT FOR OTHERS.[11]

—Notre Dame president Rev. Charles L. O'Donnell

KNUTE KENNETH ROCKNE WAS A MULTIFACETED GENIUS OF THE SORT THAT DEFIES EASY CATALOGUING. HE WAS WORLDLY YET HOMESPUN. HE WAS A RAH-RAH TEAM MAN WHO FELT AT HOME WITH SCREWBALLS AND LOSERS. AS BOTH FOOTBALL COACH AND CHEMISTRY INSTRUCTOR, HE WAS A FUNDAMENTALIST WITH A REVOLUTIONARY FLAIR. HE WAS A BRAINY, NITPICKING PERFECTIONIST WITH THE BROAD APPEAL OF A CIRCUS CLOWN.[12]

—Sports Illustrated writer Coles Phinizy

WE USED TO LOVE TO GO TO PRACTICE BECAUSE ROCK WAS
SUCH A CHARACTER. HIS PEP TALKS DEPENDED ON THE
IMPORTANCE OF THE GAME. I ONLY RECALL HIS GIVING A FEW.
ONE INVOLVED A TELEGRAM FROM HIS LITTLE BOY, BILLY,
BEFORE THE GEORGIA TECH GAME IN 1922. ROCKNE PROBABLY
SENT THE WIRE HIMSELF. HE CAME INTO THE LOCKER ROOM
WITH A BUNCH OF TELEGRAMS FROM PROMINENT ALUMNI
AND SAID TO US, "I HAVE ONE WIRE HERE, BOYS, THAT
PROBABLY DOESN'T MEAN MUCH TO YOU, BUT IT DOES TO ME.
IT'S FROM MY POOR SICK LITTLE BOY, BILLY, WHO IS
CRITICALLY ILL IN THE HOSPITAL." ROCK WAS A GREAT
ACTOR. HE GOT A LUMP IN HIS THROAT AND HIS LIPS BEGAN
TO TREMBLE AS HE READ BILLY'S WIRE: "I WANT DADDY'S
TEAM TO WIN." WE WON THE 1922 GEORGIA TECH GAME FOR
BILLY, AND WHEN WE GOT HOME WE FOUND OUT BILLY
HADN'T BEEN SICK AT ALL. THERE WAS A BIG CROWD TO MEET
US AT THE STATION, AND RUNNING AROUND IN FRONT OF
EVERYONE WAS "SICK" LITTLE BILLY ROCKNE, LOOKING
HEALTHY ENOUGH FOR A PET MILK AD.[13]

—*Four Horseman Jim Crowley*

IT IS NOT UNTRUE TO SAY THAT NO DEATH WITHIN THE
CONFINES OF THE UNITED STATES CAUSED MORE GRIEF AND
DEPRESSION IN THOSE YEARS.[14]

—a historian in 1943

HE WAS ONLY A FOOTBALL COACH, GOD REST HIS GALLANT
SOUL, BUT, HE, TOO, LED MEN AND TAUGHT THEM THE VALUE
OF HIGHER, CLEANER THINGS ALTHOUGH HIS PULPIT WAS
ONLY A PLAYING FIELD AND HIS MEDIUM ONLY A FOOTBALL.[15]

—Bill Cunningham, Boston Post

YOU'D PRACTICE 'TIL YOUR FINGERNAILS SWEAT.[16]

—Moon Mullins on playing for Rockne

WE THOUGHT IT WOULD TAKE A PRESIDENT, OR A GREAT
PUBLIC MAN'S DEATH, TO MAKE A WHOLE NATION,
REGARDLESS OF AGE, RACE, OR CREED SHAKE THEIR HEADS IN
REAL SINCERE SORROW AND SAY, "AIN'T IT A SHAME HE IS
GONE." WELL, THAT'S WHAT THIS COUNTRY DID TODAY,
KNUTE, FOR YOU. WHY, YOU OLD, BALD-HEADED RASCAL, YOU
DIED ONE OF OUR NATIONAL HEROES. NOTRE DAME WAS YOUR
ADDRESS BUT EVERY GRIDIRON IN AMERICA WAS YOUR HOME.[17]

—Will Rogers, the day after Rockne's death

HOW IS THIS FACT TO BE ACCOUNTED FOR? WHAT WAS THE SECRET OF HIS IRRESISTIBLE APPEAL TO ALL SORTS AND CONDITIONS OF MEN? WHO SHALL PLUCK OUT THE HEART OF HIS MYSTERY AND LAY BARE THE INNER SOURCE OF THE POWER HE HAD? WHEN WE SAY SIMPLY, HE WAS A GREAT AMERICAN, WE SHALL GO FAR TOWARDS SATISFYING MANY, FOR ALL OF US RECOGNIZE AND LOVE THE ATTRIBUTES OF THE TRUE AMERICAN CHARACTER. WHEN WE SAY THAT HE WAS AN INSPIRER OF YOUNG MEN IN THE DIRECTION OF HIGH IDEALS THAT WERE CONSPICUOUSLY EXEMPLIFIED IN HIS OWN LIFE, WE HAVE COVERED MUCH THAT UNQUESTIONABLY WAS TRUE OF HIM. WHEN WE LINK HIS NAME WITH THE INTRINSIC CHIVALRY AND ROMANCE OF A GREAT COLLEGE GAME, WHICH HE, PERHAPS MORE THAN ANY OTHER ONE MAN, HAS MADE FINER AND CLEANER IN ITSELF AND LARGER IN ITS POPULAR APPEAL, HERE, TOO, WE TOUCH UPON A VITAL POINT. BUT NO ONE OF THESE THINGS, NOR ALL OF THEM TOGETHER, CAN QUITE SUM UP THIS MAN WHOSE TRAGIC DEATH AT THE EARLY AGE OF FORTY-THREE HAS LEFT THE COUNTRY AGHAST. CERTAINLY, THE CIRCUMSTANCES OF HIS DEATH DO NOT FURNISH THE ANSWER. I DO NOT KNOW THE ANSWER. I WOULD NOT DARE THE IRREVERENCE OF GUESSING.[18]

—*text of Rockne eulogy by Notre Dame president Rev. Charles L. O'Donnell*

I AM NOT GOING TO BE MISSED BECAUSE THE MAN WHOM I AM RECOMMENDING AS MY SUCCESSOR WILL GO FAR BEYOND ANY SUCCESS THAT I MAY HAVE ENJOYED.[19]

—Notre Dame coach Jesse Harper on announcing his retirement in 1917

ROCKNE IS WHAT THE PSYCHOANALYSTS MIGHT CALL A "FOOTBALL COMPLEX," A BUNDLE OF INSTINCTS AND CONSCIOUS STATES GOVERNED BY A PREDOMINANT IDEA OF TURNING OUT FOOTBALL PLAYERS AND FOOTBALL TEAMS. HE LIVES AND THINKS FOOTBALL IN TERMS OF HIS EVERYDAY LIFE AND APPLIES THE SMALLEST LESSON OF HIS EXPERIENCE TO HIS FOOTBALL THEORY. HE KNOWS PSYCHOLOGY AND HE USES IT IN HIS THEORY AND PRACTICE. HE HAS A HEALTHY INTEREST IN A GREAT NUMBER OF SUBJECTS NOT CONCERNED WITH ATHLETICS, BUT HE EXTRACTS FROM THESE EXTRINSIC PURSUITS, GERMS OF HUMAN ACTION AND TENDENCY AND APPLIES THEM TO HIS ATHLETIC THEORY. HE HAS A NATURAL DRIVE AND A DYNAMIC PERSONALITY THAT IS IDEALLY SUITED TO HANDLING A SQUAD OF ATHLETES. ROCK IS BOSS OF THE FIELD—THERE IS NEVER ANY DOUBT OF THAT—BUT HIS MEN RECOGNIZE THAT ROCK UTILIZES HIS AUTHORITY ALWAYS WITH THE ONE OBJECT IN VIEW TOWARD WHICH THEY ALL ARE WORKING—THEIR OWN PERFECTION AND THE SUPERIORITY OF THE TEAM.[20]

—from the Dome *following the 1921 season*

ONCE THE GAME STARTED, ROCK SEEMED TO BE CALM
ENOUGH, BUT WHAT HE WAS, WAS THE EYE OF THE WELL-
KNOWN HURRICANE. THE MOST VISIBLE THING ABOUT HIM
WAS THE DAMNED CIGAR. HE'D TWIRL IT BETWEEN HIS
THUMB AND INDEX FINGER. OFTEN IT'D GO OUT AND HE
WOULDN'T KNOW IT. HE'D DRAW ON IT ANYWAY. AND THEN
THERE WAS HIS CONSTANT CHATTER. A RUNNING COMMENT,
NOT LOUD, SOMETIMES BARELY AUDIBLE, BUT THE STUDENT
MANAGER SITTING AT HIS FEET HAD TO BE READY, BECAUSE
ROCK WANTED CERTAIN COMMENTS TO BE JOTTED DOWN SO
HE COULD REFER TO THEM LATER.[21]

—*Four Horseman Harry Stuhldreher*

WE LOOKED TO JESSE (HARPER) FOR THE TACTICAL PLAN AND
TO ROCK FOR INSPIRATION. THEN ALL OF A SUDDEN WHEN
ROCK WAS IN CHARGE ALONE IT WAS AS IF HE HAD MATURED
OVERNIGHT. HERE HE WAS, JUST THIRTY YEARS OLD, BUT HE
HAD GREAT VISION EVEN THEN. HE WAS GROWING FAST, AND
WE KNEW IT. HE ALWAYS TOLD US TO KEEP OUR HEADS UP
AND OUR EYES OPEN, AND HE FOLLOWED HIS OWN ADVICE.[22]

—*Notre Dame quarterback Chet Grant*

AS I SIT CRUSHED AND HEARTBROKEN IN THIS LIFELESS LITTLE OFFICE WHERE KNUTE ROCKNE AND I SO OFTEN MAPPED OUT PLANS OF BATTLE—BATTLES TO FORGE WINNING FOOTBALL TEAMS AND WINNING MEN—I WONDER IF THERE LIVES A NOTRE DAME MAN WHO BELIEVES THE GREAT SPIRIT OF OUR ROCK IS DEAD. HE IS GONE FROM US, BUT HIS SPIRIT LIVES. AND WHEN WE LINE UP FOR FUTURE FIGHTS, THAT SPIRIT WILL CARRY US ON TO NEW HEIGHTS. NO, ROCKNE HAS MANY MORE VICTORIES LEFT FOR OLD NOTRE DAME. HE'LL MAKE US WIN. WHEN WE ARE BACKED TO THE WALL, IT WILL BE, "DO IT FOR ROCK, BOYS." SUCH AN INSPIRATION CANNOT BE DENIED. TO A LAST MAN, WE'LL CARRY ON.[23]

—Hunk Anderson, who succeeded Rockne

HE WAS A COMPLICATED, ENORMOUSLY AMBITIOUS MAN WHO WAS PROBABLY MORE ARTICULATE THAN ANY OTHER FIGURE EVER PRODUCED IN THE GAME. THOSE WHO HAD LISTENED TO HIS ENTREATIES, HUMOR, SARCASM, AND OCCASIONAL BULLYING SWORE THAT HE COULD TALK THE BIRDS OUT OF THE MAGNOLIAS.[24]

—author Ray Robinson

136

AS A SPORTS ANNOUNCER. I WAS TOLD BY MANY OF THE
GREAT COACHES IN THIS LAND WHOSE TEAMS HAD PLAYED
AGAINST NOTRE DAME TEAMS UNDER ROCKNE, THAT ONE OF
THEIR HARDEST PROBLEMS WHEN PLAYING NOTRE DAME WAS
THAT THEIR TEAM WORSHIPED ROCKNE—THAT THEY WERE
FANS OF HIS, AND THAT WHEN THEY CAME OUT IN THE FIELD,
THE FIRST THING THEY LOOKED FOR WAS, WHERE WAS THIS
GREAT, GREAT COACH.[25]

—former President Ronald Reagan

END NOTES

1. Robert Harron, *Rockne, Idol of American Football*, A. L. Burt Company, 1931, 98.
2. Ibid., 109.
3. Ibid., 125.
4. Michael Bonifer and L. G. Weaver, *Out of Bounds*, Piper, 1978, 60.
5. Christy Walsh, *Knute Rockne on Football*, Individual Publications, 1931, 24.
6. Ibid., 10.
7. Ibid., 24.
8. Ibid., 25.
9. Ibid., 25.
10. Ibid., 25.
11. Arthur Daley, *Knute Rockne: Football Wizard of Notre Dame*, P. J. Kenedy & Sons, 1960, 169.
12. *The Glory of Notre Dame*, Bartholomew House Ltd., 1971, 16.
13. Ibid.,135.
14. Ibid., 52.
15. Harry Stuhldreher, *Knute Rockne: Man Builder*, Macrae-Smith-Company, 1931, 176.
16. Ibid., 282.
17. Ray Robinson, *Rockne of Notre Dame*, Oxford Press, 1999, 142.
18. Michael R. Steele, *Knute Rockne: A Bio-Bibliography*, Greenwood Press, 1983, 42.
19. Harron, 21.
20. Ibid., 27.
21. Ibid., 27.
22. *Rockne of Notre Dame*, the Rockne Memorial Association, 1931, 15.
23. *Official Football Review*, 1931, 99.
24. Walsh, 8.

End Notes

25. Ibid., 35.
26. Ibid., 58.
27. Harron, 100.
28. Ibid., 124.
29. *Rockne of Notre Dame*, 109.
30. Bonifer and Weaver, 41.
31. Ibid., 53.
32. Ibid., 60.
33. Ibid., 60.
34. George Kirksey, United Press, April 1, 1931.
35. *Chicago Herald and Examiner*.
36. Walsh, 15.
37. Ibid., 18.
38. Ibid., 28.
39. Ibid., 28.
40. Ibid., 28.
41. Ibid., 52.
42. Ibid., 53.
43. Francis Wallace, *Knute Rockne*, Doubleday & Company, 1960, 123.
44. Daley, 97.
45. *Knute Rockne's Career*, Modern Magazines, 1931, 37.
46. Ibid., 38.
47. Ibid., 38.
48. Ibid., 38.
49. Stuhldreher, 12.
50. Robinson, 112.
51. H. W. Hurt, *Goals: The Life of Knute Rockne*, Murray Book Corporation, 1931, 208.
52. Kirksey.
53. Wallace.
54. Jerry Brondfield, *Rockne*, Random House, 1976, 87.
55. Ibid., 88.

56. Ibid., 90.
57. Robinson, 75.
58. Ibid., 85.
59. Patrick Chelland, *One for the Gipper*, Henry Regnery Company, 1973, 86.
60. *Knute Rockne's Career*, 32.
61. Harron, 107.
62. *Rockne of Notre Dame*, 109.
63. Walsh, 18.
64. Ibid., 14.
65. Daley, 109.
66. *The Glory of Notre Dame*, 15.
67. Ibid., 20.
68. Ibid., 49.
69. Brondfield, 122.
70. Ibid., 129.
71. Robinson, 121.
72. *Official Football Review*, 53.
73. Bonifer and Weaver, 60.
74. Kirksey.
75. Ibid.
76. Walsh, 4.
77. Ibid., 4.
78. Ibid., 4.
79. Ibid., 18.
80. Ibid., 23.
81. Ibid., 39.
82. *Knute Rockne's Career*, 38.
83. Ibid., 54.
84. Ibid., 54.
85. Harron, 70.
86. *Rockne of Notre Dame*, 110.
87. Bonifer and Weaver, 51.

End Notes

88. Ibid., 60.
89. Walsh, 13.
90. Ibid., 19.
91. Ibid., 22.
92. Ibid., 28.
93. Ibid., 79.
94. Ibid., 90.
95. *Knute Rockne's Career*, 26.
96. Ibid., 43.
97. Robinson, 131.
98. Robert Quakenbush and Mike Bynum, *Knute Rockne: His Life and Legend*, October Football Corp., 1988, 131.
99. Harron, 141.
100. Bonifer and Weaver, 60
101. Ibid., 60.
102. Ibid., 60.
103. Ibid., 60.
104. Ibid., 60.
105. Walsh, 15.
106. Ibid., 35.
107. Ibid., 35.
108. Ibid., 54.
109. Ibid., 90.
110. Ibid., 119.
111. *Knute Rockne's Career*, 30.
112. Ibid., 38.
113. Brondfield, 147.
114. Stuhldreher, 20.
115. Ibid., 155.
116. Ibid., 160.
117. Chelland, 93.
118. H. W. Hurt, 120.
119. Ibid., 207.

120. Eugene J. Young, *With Rockne at Notre Dame*, Van Rees Press, 1951, 134.
121. Ibid., 160.
122. *Rockne of Notre Dame*, 109.
123. Ibid., 109.
124. *Official Football Review*, 53.
125. Ibid., 59.
126. Bonifer and Weaver, 60.
127. Walsh, 9.
128. Ibid., 15.
129. Ibid., 27.
130. Ibid., 28.
131. Ibid., 28.
132. Ibid., 29.
133. Ibid., 35.
134. Ibid., 35.
135. Ibid., 42.
136. Ibid., 48.
137. Ibid., 57.
138. Ibid., 68
139. Ibid., 90.
140. Daley, 70.
141. *Knute Rockne's Career*, 54.
142. Brondfield, 83.
143. Ibid., 84.
144. Robinson, 143
145. Ibid., 132.
146. Quakenbush and Bynum, 132.
147. Harron, 216.
148. *Rockne of Notre Dame*, 5.
149. Bonifer and Weaver, 54.
150. Ibid., 60.
151. Ibid., 60.

End Notes

152. Ibid., 60.
153. Walsh, 4.
154. Ibid., 8.
155. Ibid., 9.
156. Ibid., 9.
157. Ibid., 11.
158. Ibid., 22.
159. Ibid., 17.
160. Ibid., 17.
161. Ibid., 17.
162. Ibid., 23.
163. Ibid., 30.
164. Ibid., 32.
165. Ibid., 33.
166. Ibid., 33.
167. Ibid., 34.
168. Ibid., 34.
169. Ibid., 35.
170. *Knute Rockne's Career*, 48.
171. Brondfield, 83.
172. Ibid., 115.
173. Stuhldreher, 160.
174. Ibid., 179.
175. Robinson, 195.
176. Steele, 90.
177. Harron, 157.
178. Walsh, 39.
179. Ibid., 43.
180. Ibid., 44.
181. Brondfield, 152.

Others on Rockne

1. Harron, 7.
2. Ibid., 9.
3. Ibid., 11.
4. Ibid., 14.
5. Ibid., 94.
6. Ibid., 172.
7. Wallace, 7.
8. *Rockne of Notre Dame*, 2.
9. Ibid., 5.
10. Ibid., 13.
11. Ibid., 13.
12. *Sports Illustrated*, Sept. 10, 1979, 100.
13. Ibid., 106.
14. CBS SportsLine.com, March 26, 2001.
15. *Official Football Review*, 1931, 63.
16. Bonifer and Weaver, 54
17. From unidentified newspaper clipping
18. Robert G. Torricelli, *In Our Own Words*, Kodansha International, 1999, 96.
19. Walsh, 8.
20. Wallace, 105.
21. Brondfield, 155.
22. Chelland, 81.
23. H. W. Hurt, 259.
24. Robinson, 5.
25. President Ronald Reagan, speech at University of Notre Dame, March 9, 1988.